COLORS OF

Spain

AA Publishing

Author: Suzanne Wales

Produced by AA Publishing

Published by AA Publishing (a trading name of Automobile Association Developments Limited, whose registered office is Fanum House, Basing View, Basingstoke, Hampshire RG21 4EA; registered number 1878835)

ISBN-10: 0-7495-4671-9
ISBN-13: 978-0-7495-4671-7

A02530

A CIP catalogue record for this book is available from the British Library.

The contents of this book are believed correct at the time of printing. Nevertheless, the publishers cannot be held responsible for any errors, omissions or for changes in the details given in this book or for the consequences of any reliance on the information provided by the same. This does not affect your statutory rights.

Layouts by Alan Gooch
Printed and bound in China

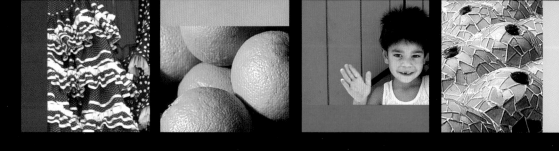

Spain

CONT

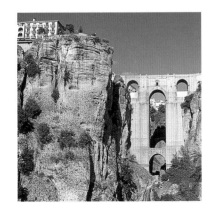

Spain is different. You have probably heard this adage dozens of times. It was coined by General Franco's tourism ministry back in the 1970s and although the dictator (as well as many of the painful memories he left behind) is long gone, the slogan has stuck. Spain (and the Spanish) are different, and immensely proud of the fact. The thing that strikes you the most is that quality is extracted from every encounter, regardless of the time it takes. Highly pragmatic and lacking in pretension, Spaniards have trouble understanding what the fuss is about. Isn't it worth lingering over a meal for an extra coffee (or three) when the company is stimulating? Why take the bus when an evening stroll is so pleasant? For the visitor, this can often be infuriating. Why, in a European country striving for cross-border "normalization," do stores and businesses still close down in the middle of the day? The *mañana* (tomorrow) attitude is alive and well, so why not put off until tomorrow what you can do today? (Especially on a day as glorious as this one.) Spend a bit of time here and you will see that these idiosyncrasies have their charming side, and you'll be seduced by the Spaniards' inherent spontaneity and love of life.

Provincial pride

The nineteen autonomous communities of Spain make a fascinating patchwork of culture and geography. When Queen Isabella and King Ferdinand "The Catholic Monarchs" united Spain in 1492, they did nothing to suppress the local pride that spread throughout the peninsula (in fact, many would argue that they only added to its strength). In vastly rural medieval Spain, the *pueblo* (village) was an entire world. This concept has stuck. Ask someone where they come from and they will first name their village, then region. The answer "Spain" will come last.

Whether out on the soccer field or in the Spanish parliament, local interests, language, and culture are defended to the hilt. Outsiders may see this as regionalism gone mad, but when you consider that Basques, Catalans, and Galicians speak a language (not a dialect) different from Castilian Spanish; that southern Spain was ruled for centuries by the Moors, that the west was colonized by the Celts, and the north has more in common with Provençal France than with central Spain—you can understand why the Spaniards are keen to dispel the clichés of what is perceived as their "national" character.

Provincial pride has many faces. It is seen in the Catalan flag-waving frenzy of 11 September—the day in 1714 when the city of Barcelona was beaten by Franco-Spanish troops in the War of Succession—and the Madrileño *castizos* (dandies) strutting their stuff along the Gran Via. It is heard in the cheers of an entire village turning out to support a game of *pelota vasca* (a Basque ballgame) or a display of stirring Galician bagpipes.

But you will probably come across it most in everyday transactions. Whether you are talking to a Galician, Catalan, or Castilian be prepared to agree that their wine is best, their weather the fairest, and their country God's own. Much of this is said with tongue firmly in cheek (and provides fuel for countless arguments and discourses), but don't brush it off lightly. If you do, you will lose the opportunity to discover the melting pot that is Spain.

Food and produce

Even if you are just in Spain on a weekend break, for a microcosm of Spanish life—and a glimpse of how important the art of eating is—head to a local market. Among the displays of plump peaches, curly heads of lettuce, piles of seafood packed on ice, and freshly killed game hanging in rows above your head, you will hear the vendors waxing lyrical about their produce. Tomatoes are *guapa* (attractive), prawns *frescísimas* (fresher than fresh) and a potato *maca* (congenial), suggesting that you might be able to have a pleasant conversation with one were it able to talk. The adoration of food and the right to eat well spans all classes and ages, with even 12-year-olds able to distinguish between a regular slice of *jamón serrano* (cured ham) and its superior cousin the *pata negra* (black hoof). Basque taxi drivers are one of the best sources of knowledge on their region's numerous five-star restaurants, so be prepared to talk truffles in the cab from the airport.

When dining, the Spanish do it like no other nation. The two-hour lunch break is often spent bonding with co-workers over a three-course *menu del día* in a local tavern, and no Sunday is complete without fish, whether it is cod cooked at home in the oven or a full meal in an upscale restaurant overlooking the sea. Although most people will claim that no one can make a tortilla like

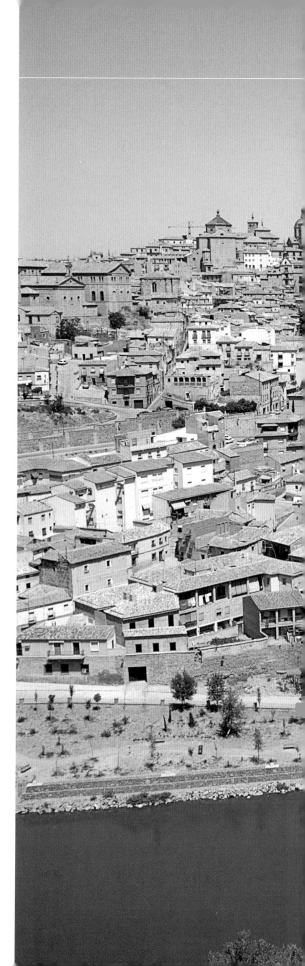

The city of Toledo in central Spain is set on a hilltop in a narrow loop of the river Tagus.

their own mother, new-wave chefs are putting Spain at the forefront of cutting-edge cuisine. Spain has more bars per head than anywhere else in Europe and the art of *el tapeo*, tapas bar hopping, is a Saturday night pastime.

Despite the proliferation of hothouse agriculture, seasonality reigns. If you visit in the fall, expect to eat fungi and snails; in spring, marvel at the plumpness and flavor of tomatoes. Again, the market is the best place to appreciate this changing cornucopia. Just dive on in.

Fiestas

In the sixteenth century, when the rest of Europe was enjoying a Renaissance, Spain was hanging on stoically to "dark age" Catholicism and its rights and rituals designed to pacify a restless population. During the following centuries, and partly in fear of losing its distinctiveness from its neighbors, religious fervor gained even more momentum. But this only goes some way towards explaining the sheer number of the country's fiestas; the rest can be put down to a love of fun, getting together, and *desmadre*, a term that loosely means "letting it all hang out." Nothing can quite describe the experience of stumbling into a small village to see the entire population out and about, in streets decorated to honor a local saint or some historical event that, if it weren't for the fiesta, would have lost its significance generations ago.

Spanish fiestas range from the sanctimonious to the downright bizarre. What could be further from the solemn *Semana Santa* (Holy Week) parades of the south than the heart-pumping bull running of the north? Many local clubs and organizations work all year on the decorations, only to destroy them on fiesta night. Fire, especially along the Mediterranean coastline, plays a big part. Every March in Valencia, a cheering crowd sets a match to the *fallas*, enormous effigies of popular (and not so popular) politicians, folkloric characters, and other assorted heroes and villains. The origins of *correfoc*, a hair-raising, close-encounter display of fire-breathing dragons and mischievous devils enjoyed by young and old, have been lost in antiquity, but would be banned outright in most other countries. And what are those men doing jumping over those babies lying on a mattress in Burgos? Someone, somewhere in the past said it was a cure for hernia. Or what about the "human castles" in Catalonia, where the *castellers* form pyramids that can be nine people high? It's all to do with becoming one with the earth and fellow man.

Artists and heroes

Cervantes's novel *Don Quixote* (which many consider to be the first written in the Spanish language), has left us with more than images of the warrior of the windmill-dotted plains of La Mancha, fighting his demons against all odds. It has given the English language the term "quixotic," meaning a mixture of idealism and impracticality, pride and resourcefulness. Surely these same traits ran in the blood of musician Joan Manuel Serrat who defied General Franco by singing in public in his native Catalan? Or Christopher Columbus (if he was indeed Spanish—the debate continues) when he set out to discover the New World?

More recently Baltasar Garzón, the country's crusading judge, has risked life and limb, and sometimes reputation to bring terrorists and war criminals to trial. But lionization is not solely a male domain in Spain. Take Cristina Sanchez, the only modern-day female bullfighter to attain the honor of matador or Agustina de Aragón, the feisty soldier's wife who fired a decisive canon at Napoleon's troops during the War of Independence. This incident was immortaized by painter by Francisco Goya in his emotive series the *Disasters of War*. Spain's turbulent history has often been the subject of its greatest artists. Pablo Picasso, who went into self-imposed exile in France during the Civil War, painted *Guernica*, the ultimate anti-war statement, and many of Miró's whimsical works are abstractions of Franco's cruel regime.

But Spanish art is not solely political. Among the molten clocks and skeletal trees of Salvador Dalí's dreamscapes, there are many references to the azure waters and rocky cliffs of the Costa Brava, and Catalonia's Olot school rivaled the French Impressionists in their idealized portrayal of the countryside and its bewitching light.

In real quixotic fashion, many of the country's true prodigals are names that resound only within its borders; the thousands of people who spent years fighting fascism, either on the fields or, more clandestinely, during the thirty six years of dictatorship and the scores of activists and political players who helped shape the "transition" (as it is known) and Spain's entry into the modern world. To these people Spain gives thanks for making it the passionate, vital, and liberal nation it is today.

Chimneys and ventilators on the rooftops of Casa Mila, an apartment building in Barcelona that was designed by Gaudí at the very beginning of the twentieth century.

Land and sea

Venture out of the cities on any Sunday morning and, after you have beaten the traffic jams, the hills (and valleys, coasts, and plains) will be populated by scores of *domingueros*. These "Sunday people" are cyclists exploring the mountains of Asturias, cross-generational families skirting the sierras around Madrid, sun worshippers on the Costa del Sol, and groups of everyday people who have come to enjoy the natural beauty at their doorstep. They may be heading to a seaside restaurant for Sunday paella, or to the mountains for a hearty lunch of local meat delicacies. They will think nothing of spending an extra hour or two traveling to find the place that reportedly serves the best sardines, the most succulent rabbit, the most flavorsome stews, and where the wine is produced by the owner's grandfather down the road. They will drink to his health and count their blessings, content in the knowledge that in modern-day Europe, Spain still values simple pleasures—and the most pleasurable of all is a good meal in the open air.

De tierra or *del mar*: from the land or the sea. In Spain, this says it all. A person from the land not only has his roots there but is earthy and wholesome, while "sea" people have (inherently it is presumed) a knowledge of the ocean and all that lies in it. (There is no grey area; this even applies to coastal city slickers). Food, art, character, and architecture can all fall into either category, often classified on instinct rather than by any obvious connection.

From the long sandy stretches of the beaches of the south to the rugged northern coasts, the inland deserts to the lush sierras, *tierra* and *mar* are the sanctified pillars of Spain. So take as much in as you can. As the national song *Viva España* says, everybody cries when they have to leave.

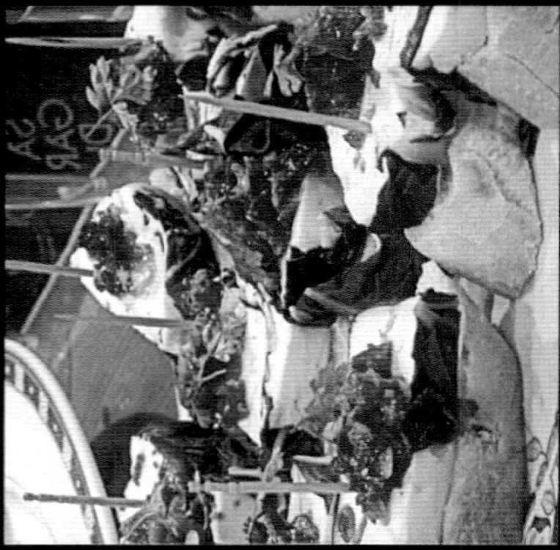

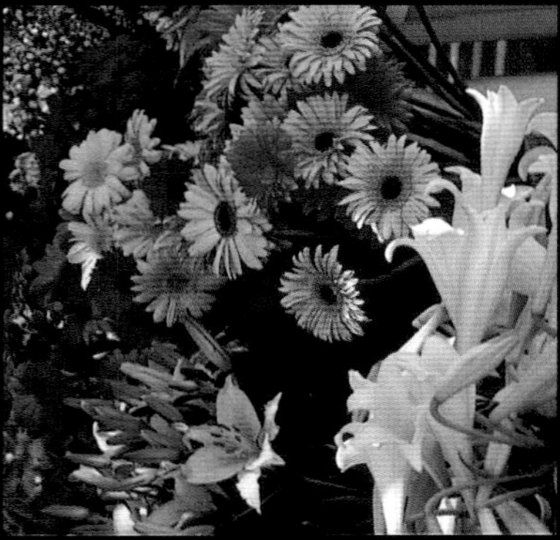

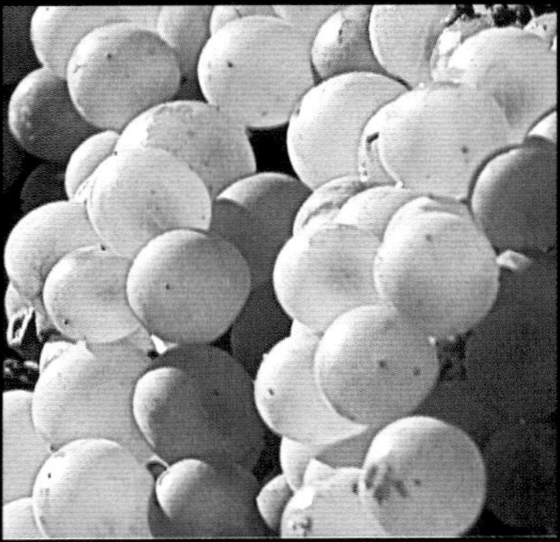

SPANISH WINE

The true flavors of Spain are found not in the fancy restaurants of Barcelona and Madrid, but in the everyday: in village bistros and portside cafés, and in the lively food markets—every city, town, and village has at least one; in the sun-baked olive groves of Jaén and among the legendary vineyards of La Rioja. Food is the heart and soul of the country and it is the foundation for every aspect of Spanish social life.

Spain's culinary tradition is steeped in history, influenced by numerous invasions and pilgrimages. The Moors brought oranges, almonds, and rice; the Romans olives and wine, while Columbus brought back tomatoes, potatoes, and peppers from the New World. The result is a cuisine that is as warm and varied as the country itself. *Buen provecho*.

The first wines in Spain were made more than two thousand years ago, and with more hectares of vineyards than anywhere else on earth, it is little surprise that Spain is now one of the world's leading wine producers.

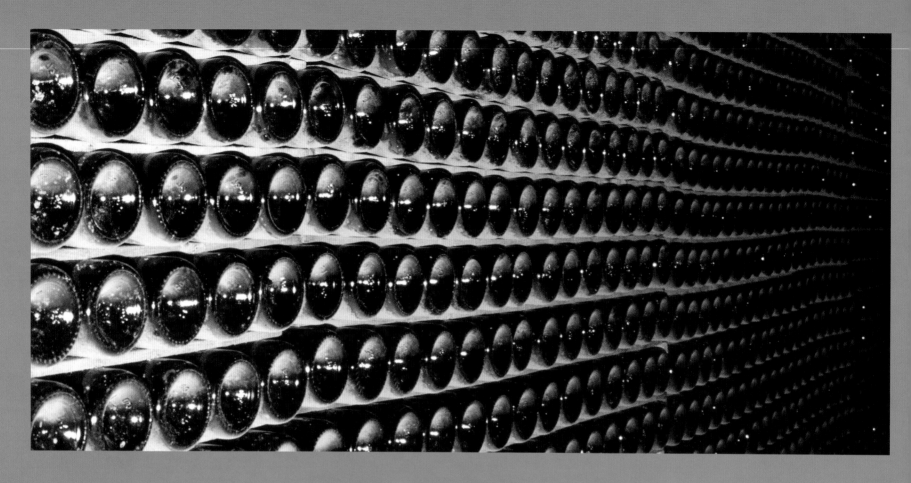

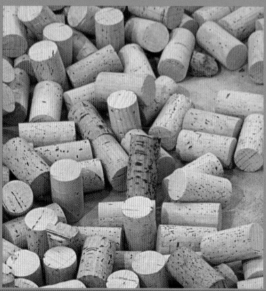

The deep reds of the Ribera del Duero, crisp *albariños* from Galicia, sherries from Andalucía, and sparkling wine from Catalonia are all justly famous for their unique ability to reflect the land they come from. Connoisseurs are keeping an eye on emerging regions too, such as Toro and Rueda.

MARKETS

Nowhere in the world are fresh produce markets more colorful or spectacular than on the Iberian Peninsula, where daily shopping for food is still an integral part of life. Displays change according to the season, and chefs do their morning rounds searching for inspiration for the day's menu.

If paella is Spain's national dish then tapas is the national "sport," a centuries-old tradition that all started, according to lore, when King Alfonso X stopped by a tavern near Cadiz in search of refreshment. As was traditional, a small slice of bread was placed over his glass of wine to keep flies out and, being a royal customer, it was topped with a slice of ham and a hunk of cheese. So tapas was born and even today in the southern regions these delightful bite-sized snacks are handed out free with drinks. To drink wine without food is unthinkable in Spain.

SEAFOOD

Spain is almost an island, with sea on all sides; the Mediterranean on the east and south, the Atlantic to the west, the Cantabrian to the north. Galicia and Asturias are famed for crustaceans and shellfish, the Basque Country for its *angulas* (baby eels) and the Andalucíans fry fish like no others.

Paella; *pa amb tomaquet*—the ubiquitous snack of
bread rubbed with ripe tomato and drizzled with
olive oil; *crema Catalana*—vanilla custard with a
burnt sugar topping; juicy, fat salted anchovies;
acorn-fed *jamón* (ham); all form part of Spain's
gastronomic heritage.

OLIVES & OAKS

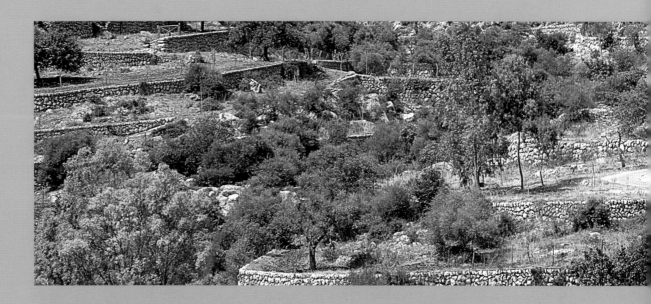

Spain has more olive groves than anywhere else in the world, boasting more than two hundred different varieties. Out of those only twenty four are used for making oil; rich, smooth, and in a kaleidoscope of flavors and aromas. Sharp green *Picual* olives from Jaén in Andalucía account for about 40 percent of the production, but others include the tiny, earthy *Arbequina* from Catalonia and sweet *Hojiblancas* that are grown on the northern slopes of Malaga. The spongy bark of the cork oak (left) is stripped to make corks for the wine industry.

LIFE &
PEOPLE

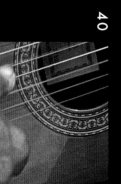

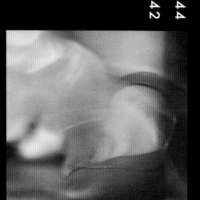

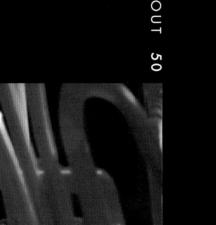

SPANISH GUITAR

Who are the Spaniards? What makes them typically Spanish? Pose this question to a Catalan or Basque and they will tell you it is their fierce nationalism, and may add that they are not "Spanish" at all. Andalucían culture (influenced by centuries of Moorish occupation), is about as far away from the Celtic myths and heroes of the Galicians as Australia is to Scotland. From island to inland dwellers, the Spanish personality is as diverse as its landscape, a shock to many visitors who arrive expecting to find the "sun, sand, and sangria" cliché everywhere.

There is however one trait that is common to all Spaniards: *individualismo* or individualism, the blessed desire to live, let live, and honor "difference" in yourself and others. It means people of all ages and classes having a drink in a square or coming together for a fiesta. In these fast, modern times, it breeds a die-hard respect for tradition.

In the mid 1800s, craftsman Antonio de Torres (1817–1892) created the Spanish guitar, known as the worlds' first "classical" guitar. So perfect was his concept, that little has changed in its design. Today it forms the backbone of flamenco music.

FLAMENCO

The origins of flamenco are still widely debated (as are those of Spain's gypsies themselves). Moorish influence is heard in the passionate cries of the *cante jondo* (deep song), as are Sephardic Jewish origins in some of the more lyrical *fandangos*.

CELEBRATE

Whether honoring a saint or an historical event, respect for tradition unites communities. Fiestas and celebrations differ wildly from province to province and even the tiniest village has its own unique way of celebrating, drawing on its own individual culture.

Above: Every Sunday people perform the Sardana, the Catalan national dance, in front of the cathedral in Barcelona.
Opposite: Folk groups gather at the Fiesta Romera held in May in Santa Cruz de Tenerife.

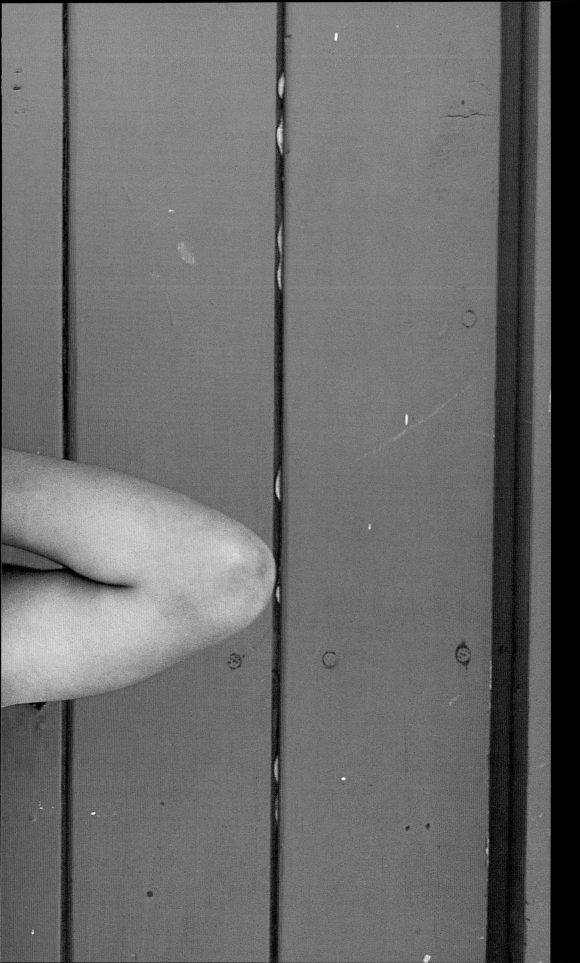

CHILDREN

Children are not shunned in Spanish society. On the contrary, many outsiders are shocked to see how much they participate in everyday "adult" life, staying up late along with their parents or hanging around the workplace learning the ropes for what may be their future profession.

TIME OUT

On average, the Spanish sleep one hour less than other Europeans and you can bet, at least on a hot evening, that much of this time is spent shooting the breeze on an outdoor *terraza*. During the day, this *terraza* provides shade and an ideal place to meet up with friends.

CROWDS

In a country that enjoys more hours of sunlight
than any other on the continent, outdoor activities
reign. *Paseando* (strolling) is a national pastime,
and sporting events, such as soccer or the bullfight,
draw enormous crowds despite the heat.

RELIGION

Even though the number of churchgoing Spaniards is falling dramatically, signs of Catholicism, particularly in the south, are everywhere. Being chosen to carry the saint during *Semana Santa* (Holy Week) processions is considered an honor.

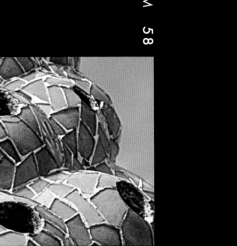

GAUDI &
MODERNISM

From the white villages of the south to the monumental castles of the great *meseta* (inland plains), soaring cathedrals, and Moorish remains, Spain's vernacular architecture inspires and intrigues. Local masters include Antoní Gaudí, the genius behind Barcelona's *modernista* movement that transformed the "new" city of the late nineteenth century with its whimsical vision. A contemporary renaissance is taking place with the work of local talents Santiago Calatrava and Rafael Moneo, while top international names such as Sir Norman Foster and Frank Gehry are competing for projects in a country fast gathering an international reputation for cutting-edge architecture.

It's been attacked by anarchists, called the ugliest building in the world (by writer George Orwell), and been the subject of scorn of local architects and historians, but that hasn't stopped work continuing on Gaudí's great unfinished symphony (and resting place) the Temple of the Sagrada Família. Expected completion date: 2026.

Barcelona's *modernista* (Art Nouveau) architects were obsessed with detail. Why leave a surface bare when it could be embellished? One of the most popular (and painstaking) techniques was *trencadis*—mosaic work using broken ceramics.

Gothic cathedrals with flying buttresses, soaring spires, and stained-glass windows were built during Spain's Golden Age (the fifteenth and sixteenth centuries), many on former Roman or Moorish sacred sites. Seville's cathedral planners said: "Let us put up a building so immense that the rest of the world will think us mad."

Above: The cathedral in Santiago de Compostela in Galicia, has elements which date back to 1075.

Far right, top: Seville's great cathedral.

Although small and unremarkable in design, the church of El Rocio in Huelva (above) is one of the most famous in Spain. Every Pentecost, thousands of pilgrims come from all over the country to honor its saint. Almost deserted throughout the rest of the year, this tiny outpost then plays host to a week-long frenzy of flamenco and religious fervor.

The court of the Mexuar in the medieval Moorish palace of the Alhambra in Granada has an intricately carved ceiling. The building was completed in 1365 and the reigning sultan received petitioners and held meetings here. Next page: the *Mezquita* (mosque) in Cordoba.

Eight centuries of Moorish culture in Iberia left behind the *Mudejar* style of perfect arches and intricate wood and plaster carvings. The ultimate examples are Cordoba's mosque and Granada's Alhambra; many forms and motifs are employed by Spain's artisans today, particularly by ceramicists.

The focal point of Spanish cities are the *plazas majors*. Over the centuries they have been used for events and gatherings such as bullfights, trials, concerts, weddings, and executions. Today they act as a recreational hub and a place to leave behind the congestion of the narrow surrounding streets.

The Plaza de España (left and above), is Seville's
plaza major, bounded by an artificial river or moat.
Next page: The white village of Casares de las
Hurdes in the province of Extremadura.

Museums are the dream project for top architects, and mayors wishing to endow their cities with keynote buildings. Gehry's Guggenheim in Bilbao not only gave the city its first major museum, but also managed to transform it from industrial backwater to major tourist destination.

LANDMA
& VIEWS

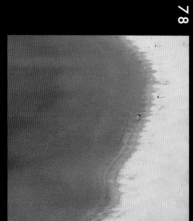

ARKS

4

COLORS OF SPAIN:
LANDMARKS & VIEWS

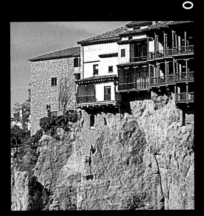

LA PLAYA

Spain is the second largest country in Western Europe, covering a surface area of nearly 200,000 square miles. It has pine forests and river deltas, mountains and deserts, obscure fishing villages and cosmopolitan cities, and 2,466 miles of coastline. Spain's territory includes the Balearic Islands with their laid-back lifestyle, the windswept Canary Islands of the Atlantic, and the towns of Melilla and Ceuta on the North African coast. The bucket-and-spade tourist resorts of General Franco's Spain barely scratch the surface.

Historically Spain has been invaded and conquered, reconquered, and liberated— reflected in its art and architecture in the form of majestic Roman aqueducts and theaters, Moorish *pueblos blancos* with pretty, cobbled streets, and the windmills of central Spain immortalized by Cervantes's Don Quixote. Contemporary Spain meanwhile attracts hordes of artists and architects all eager to put their mark on the land, while the Mediterranean sea, once the domain of fishing boats and pirates, has become a playground for watersports enthusiasts.

From the Costa Blanca, named for its white sand, the Costa Brava for its rugged cliffs, the Costa de la Luz for its magical light, to the Costa Verde for its green countryside, the Spanish Costas (thirteen in all, including the islands), provide everything from beach bars and parties to near prehistoric seclusion.

PORTS

The life force of the coastal areas, many of these small, seemingly unimportant harbor towns have sustained fishermen and their families for generations and have changed little. Larger ports, such as that in Cadiz where Francis Drake famously sank thirty vessels of the Spanish Armada in the middle of the fourteenth century, and the port of Palos de la Frontera, in Huelva province, where Columbus set sail on his voyage to the New World, played an important role in shaping Spain's destiny.

Other ports, like Barcelona's Port Vell and Marbella's Puerto Banus are stomping grounds for the rich and glamorous, as much a part of the show as any bullfight or *zarzuela* (Spanish opera). Pirates and buccaneers no longer being a problem, these seaside playgrounds are a-buzz with lively cafés and excellent fish restaurants. Some have been transformed by art, as can be seen in the candy-colored concrete cubes of "Los Cubos de la Memoria" at Llanes Harbor in Asturias (above). Next page: High-rise hotels dominate the coastline at Benidorm on the Costa Blanca.

The Sierra Nevada in Granada is the undulating rooftop of Spain, rising to the magnificent height of 11,424 feet at Mulhacen. This is the highest point in the country and the only place in the world where you can ski with a sea view. To the north, the mighty Pyrenees and the Picos de Europa (left) form a natural frontier between Spain and France, offering jagged, fairytale peaks to serious hikers.

Previous page: Sunset over the Roque Bentaiga mountain range on the island of Gran Canaria.

The ancient town of Ronda in Andalucía (above) is
one of the oldest cities in Spain, ruled first by the
Celts, then the Phoenicians, then the Romans.
Today it's a center for bullfighting, teetering madly
on the brink of the 330-feet deep El Tajo and
marks the heart of the region's *pueblos blancos*.

Elsewhere, the secluded hamlets of the Pyrenees
and the north are surrounded by ancient volcanoes
and fast rivers. The rock formations of the *meseta*
(plains) of Central Spain are a backdrop to the
famed *casas colgadas* (hanging houses) of Cuenca,
earning it the nickname "the Venice of the Air."

CASTLES & WINDMILLS

Some of Spain's finest monuments to rural life are the small hilltop towns and villages heaped on top of one another. Presided over by castles and windmills, and clinging to the edge of a canyon or the top of a hill, these strategic hamlets were first conceived as lookout posts against attack.

Above: The fifteenth-century castle at Manzanares El Real in Andalucía. Top: The circular courtyard at Bellver Castle in Palma on the island of Mallorca. Above right: Crenellated stone walls curving around the fifteenth-century castle of Belmonte in Cuenca province.

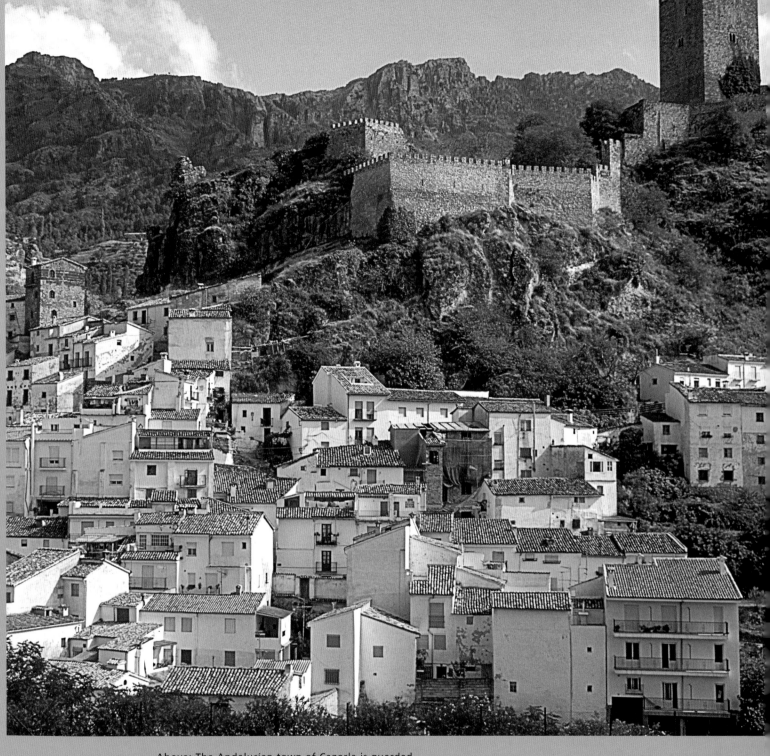

Above: The Andalucían town of Cazorla is guarded by the Moorish castle of La Yedra. Left: Slate-roofed turrets at the fortress in Segovia.
Next page: Windmills at Consuegra, not far from from the city of Toledo.

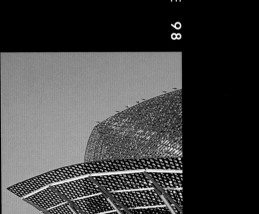

COLORS OF SPAIN:
ART, CULTURE, & STYLE

5

AVANT-GARDE

Salvador Dalí, Pablo Picasso, Joan Miró; many Spanish names are at the forefront of breakthrough artistic styles. Back in the sixteenth century, El Greco painted the suffering underclasses in dreamlike imagery and Velázquez was probably the most famous court painter of all time. Today, abstract expressionists Antoni Tápies and Miquel Barceló are known as the new masters and contemporary Spanish designers such as Oscar Tusquets and Javier Mariscal export "Spanish Style" all over the planet.

Spanish art and style is exuberant and bold. Barcelona is known as an international design city and a renaissance in cuisine and cinema (the latter with Pedro Almodóvar at the helm) is making headlines the world over. After the years of dictatorship, when the arts (and artists) were stifled, and with a liberal government at the helm, the arts are booming. Not that the traditional is shunned: old-school imagery and artisan techniques sit effortlessly alongside the avant-garde.

Although he spent much of his life abroad, Salvador Dalí was first and foremost a Catalan. His most eccentric work is a museum in his otherwise nondescript hometown of Figueres in northern Catalonia; a former theater crowned with eggs and covered with loaves of bread.

Tourism is Spain's biggest industry, and hotels have become the new bastions of style. Boutique hotels and hip hostelries are replacing the package-tourist monstrosities of the boom years of the sixties and seventies. The Hotel Arts in Barcelona (above) is a prime example.

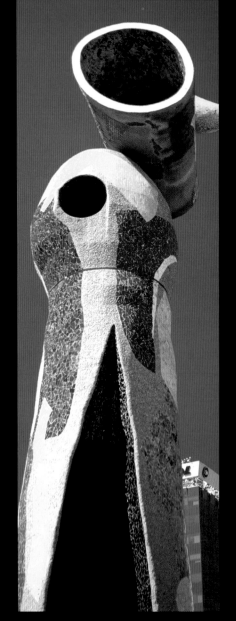

Vibrant street art and sculpture contrasts with
weathered stone walls in major cities. Barcelona
set the trend. In preparation for the 1992
Olympic Games, works by international artists
were commissioned to grace the city's newly
constructed plazas, parks, and promenades.

THE BULLFIGHT

Love or loathe the spectacle, no one can deny the elegance of the bullfighter in full regalia. His *traje de luces* (suit of lights) has been his glittering armor since the seventeenth century. Only a fully fledged *matador* is entitled to have his suit embroidered in gold.

Spain cannot be credited with inventing the fan
(its origins can be traced to ancient Roman and
Asian cultures), but no other European country
uses it as much. It is also a part of the flamenco
costume, along with swirling, flounced dresses
and embroidered shawls.

FLAMENCO STYLE

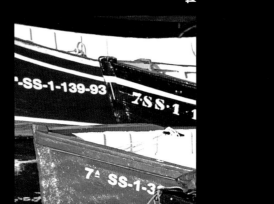

SEEING RED

An old Spanish proverb says *de sol de tarde, Dios te guarde* (in the afternoon sun, the lord watches over you). There is little doubt that the Spanish are supreme sun worshippers (perhaps the sun god Apollo never left with the Romans), but the nuances of the day's light change the colors and reflections of Spain in infinite ways during its cycle. After rising over the Balearic Islands in the east and before setting at Finisterre (Land's End), the peninsula's westernmost point, the sun creates dramatic early morning shadows over the northern mountains, shimmering reflections of everyday life in the city's fountains, and sends southerners to their siesta in the heat of the afternoon.

At night, artificial light, whether bulb or candle, casts shadows on ancient stone walls, highlighting intricate architectural details, or illuminating the faces of a pair of diners. In Spain, the expression "seeing the light" takes on a whole new meaning.

Viva la vida roja. Red is the color often associated with Spain. The shade of flamenco and bullfights, it is brash, sexy, brave—with a hint of danger. It is everywhere, from caves at Arta in Mallorca (above) to a blood-red sunset at the old pirate enclave of El Charco de San Gines in Lanzarote (right).

DUSK

The harsh light of day gives way to the vibrant blues, pinks, and violets of dusk. This is a magical time along the Mediterranean seaboard, when people take a coastal promenade or seek out a spot to enjoy the view.

URBAN OASIS

Even in the cities, water is not too far away.
Contemporary architects have created modern
oases with artificial lakes and ponds that reflect
their urban surroundings. The Parc de l'Espanya
Industrial in Barcelona (right) celebrates the city's
manufacturing and commercial heritage.

THE OCEAN

The mighty Atlantic ocean batters Spain's western coast and the Canary Islands, where the color of the sand (above) reflects Tenerife's volcanic activity. At Finisterre in Galicia (right), waves lap the spectacular Costa da Morte (Coast of Death), named for its fatal toll on the local fishing population.

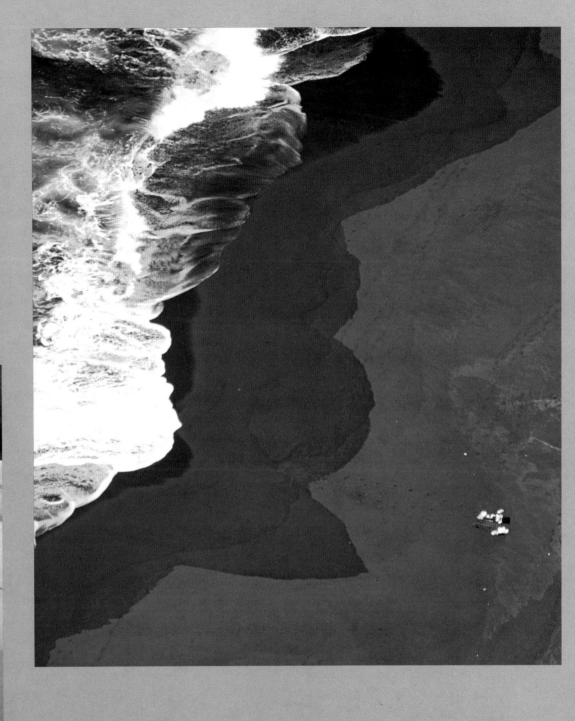

Pleasure vessels abound in the coastal marinas of
the Mediterranean, with Malaga and Mallorca the
most exclusive mooring spots. The latter is the King
of Spain's preferred port—he races there every year
in his namesake regatta. However, Valencia, host
of the 2007 America's Cup, is running a close third.

SET SAIL

Weathered boats, the vessels of Spain's artisan fishermen, bob in the fishing ports. Even against stiff competition from industrial fishing fleets, forty thousand people still fish the surrounding seas using centuries-old methods to bait octopus, crab, and a cornucopia of edible marine creatures.

EVENING GLOW

In Spain, 2 percent of the overall electricity
consumption is spent on floodlighting public
monuments. Modern architecture, Gothic cathedrals
and *modernista* follies take on a different light
under an inky sky thanks to clever illumination.
Previous pages: The port at Malaga.

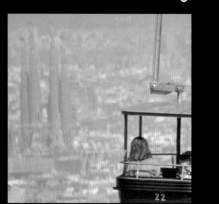

FIESTA 142

TAXIS

Spain's first taxi services were run by *gremios*, forerunners to trade unions that flourished in Barcelona in the Middle Ages. Today the four-wheeled varieties take people to and from work and play, while tourists tend to prefer the more traditional versions.

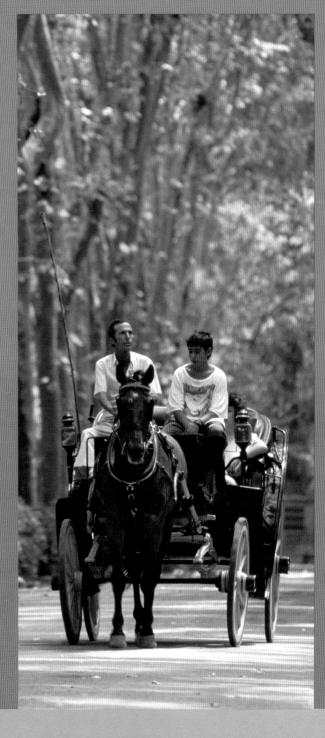

ON THE ROAD

It's been a long time coming but Spain's love of
four wheels is being replaced by a love of two. In
the traffic-locked cities, bicycles and motorcycles
are a convenient way to get around and weekend
cycling has become a popular pastime, especially
in the mountains in the north.

Hair-raising, sky-high thrills give participants a panoramic view of the skyline and surrounding countryside, at a frantic, "don't-blink-or-you'll-miss-it" pace. This rollercoaster is at the Parc d'Atraccions Tibidabo in Barcelona, on a hill high above the city.

A relaxed, bird's-eye view of a city is the best way
to appreciate its history through urban contrasts.
Ancient towns morph into modern residential
suburbs and on to industrial peripheries. Cable cars
in Barcelona take visitors to the top of Montjuïc.
Next pages: La Gomera in the Canary Islands.

Fire plays an important role in the all-night fiestas held along the Mediterranean coast. The biggest are Valencia's *fallas*, Catalonia's *correfoc* (fire run) and San Juan, the celebration of the summer solstice that traditionally ends with a cooling dip in the sea at sunrise.

CREDITS

The photographs used in this book are held in the Automobile Association's own photo library (**AA World Travel Library**) and were taken by the following photographers:

Peter Baker back cover center left, 3cl, 4l, 19bl, 28/9, 32r; **Pete Bennett** 46cb, 84br, 85c, 137bl; **Michelle Chaplow** front cover bottom, back cover center right, 3cr, 10t, 10b, 18bc, 18br, 19bc, 22bl, 24l, 26tc, 27tc, 27tr, 27br, 31cl, 31cr, 31r, 34tl, 34bl, 34bc, 37b, 38bl, 38br, 40/1, 47bl, 47br, 48/9, 58l, 60tl, 60bl, 61br, 67bc, 67br, 68/9, 70, 71tl, 77l, 77c, 82/3, 84tl, 91, 93r, 94/5, 96l, 96c, 97r, 99, 100r, 102tl, 103cl, 103br, 109, 112tl, 112tr, 112cr, 112br, 113tr, 113bl, 124, 126/7, 128bl, 134r, 135, 141cr; **Steve Day** front cover top, 5r, 14/5, 16/7, 44, 58br, 59, 60tr, 100l, 114r, 115r, 120/1, 128tl, 128r, 129, 130r, 136, 137; **Jerry Edmanson** 8/9, 19br, 26cl, 30/1, 33, 36, 39bl, 50/1, 65br, 67tc, 71cr, 77r, 92tl, 92/3, 108/9, 112c, 112bl, 113tc, 113cl, 140tl, 140tr, 140bl, 141tl; **Philip Enticknap** 47tl, 47tr, 50, 54r, 73, 76r, 88, 92bl, 93tl, 122/3b, 141br; **Caroline Jones** 76l, 79, 85tl, 85bl, 138/9; **Max Jourdan** back

cover right, 3r, 4c, 4r, 5cl, 5cf, 8, 22br, 23r, 25, 26cr, 27tl, 34r, 38bc, 39bc, 40b, 42/3, 42bl, 42br, 43bl, 46cl, 52, 53, 54l, 55r, 56l, 57l, 57c, 58tr, 60c, 61bc, 62r, 63, 65l, 71cl, 74, 74/5, 84bc, 85tr, 96r, 100cr, 101, 106, 107t, 107b, 115c, 125r, 130c, 132, 134tl, 134bl, 140c, 143l, 143r; **Simon McBride** back cover left, 3l, 23tl, 61cl, 97l, 102tr, 102cl, 102bc, 103bc, 110/1; **Eric Meacher** 35; **Andrew Molyneux** 34tc, 67tl, 112cl, 133r; **Rob Moore** 11, 40t, 45; **Ken Paterson** 24r, 61tl, 61tr, 92tc, 100cl, 104/5, 116/7, 144; **Jens Poulsen** 37t, 39br, 46tc, 55l; **Douglas Robertson** 12/3, 21l, 32l, 56r, 66, 67bl, 142l; **Clive Sawyer** 46cr, 46br, 78, 86/7, 114l, 117, 125l; **James Tims** 6, 67tr, 72/3, 76c, 80, 103tl, 114c, 115l, 118/9, 122, 123, 130l, 133l, 140/1; **Wyn Voysey** 26bc; **Rick Strange** 23bl, 103tr; **Steve Watkins** 18bl, 20, 21r, 64, 81, 84tc, 85br, 89, 98, 131l, 142r; **Peter Wilson** 5l, 22t, 47bc, 56c, 62l, 65tr, 90/1, 118b.